Workbook

---

for

Beyond Order:

12 More Rules for Life

By Jordan B. Peterson

Genius Reads

Legal & Disclaimer

The information contained in this book and its contents is not designed to replace or take the place of any form of medical or professional advice; and is not meant to replace the need for independent medical, financial, legal, or other professional advice or services, as may be required. The content and information in this book have been provided for educational and entertainment purposes only.

The content and information contained in this book have been compiled from sources deemed reliable, and it is accurate to the best of the Author's knowledge, information, and belief. However, the Author cannot guarantee its accuracy and validity and cannot be held liable for any errors and/or omissions. Further, changes are periodically made to this book as and when needed. Where appropriate and/or necessary, you must consult a professional (including but not limited to your doctor, attorney, financial advisor, or such other professional advisor) before using any of the suggested remedies, techniques, or information in this book.

Upon using the contents and information contained in this book, you agree to hold harmless the Author from and against any damages, costs, and expenses, including any legal fees potentially resulting from the application of any of the information provided by this book. This disclaimer applies to any loss, damages, or injury caused by the use and application,

Download Your Free Gift

Before you go any further, why not pick up a free gift from me to you?

Smarter Brain – a 10-part video training series to help you develop higher IQ, memory, and creativity – FAST!

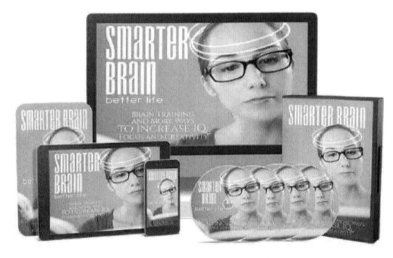

www.Geniusreads.com

Table of Contents

Introduction

Beyond Order is the follow up to Jordan Peterson's international bestseller *12 Rules for Life*. Following an illustrious career in clinical psychology and a professorship at the University of Toronto both of which he continues, Peterson's sometimes controversial approach to the ills of modern life has garnered him widespread support and condemnation from some sections of society. This combination has led, not only to a great amount of exposure, world press tours, and well-publicized cancellation of talks at university lecture halls but to a career that has spread beyond academic psychology to popular discourse, as is exemplified by his engagement with social media and podcasting.

At first glance, this book is a follow-up to his *12 Rules for Life*. But as Peterson himself explains, it is a form of reiteration and expansion on the themes he touched on in the first book. There are certain guiding principles that Peterson is keen to get across, namely: personal responsibility, understanding of the role of conservatism and liberalism as interdependent forces, the power of memory, and the dangers of dogmatic thinking.

What cannot be captured in this workbook is the mastery of Peterson's sometimes artistic and eloquent style. His points are simple but he creates context and mythos around each of them, putting them squarely in the western canon of art, philosophy, and literature. At the same time, he draws on his many years of clinical psychology and shares insights into some of the cases he has dealt with and how they have been resolved. Also within the book are a series of images that has personally selected to preface each chapter, some of which he remarks upon in the text. These are (or are adaptations of):

1. *The Fool* from the Rider-Waite Tarot Deck
2. *Materia Prima* from the *Occulta philosophia* (1613)
3. *St George and the Dragon* by Paolo Ucecello
4. *Atlas and the Hesperides* by John Singer Sargent
5. *Fallen Angel* by Alexandre Cabanel
6. *In Our Communal Farm* by B. Deykin
7. *Apprentice* by Louis-Emile Adan
8. *Irises* by Vincent Van Gogh
9. *The Temptation of St Anthony* by Martin Schongauer
10. *The Love Drink* by Aubrey Beardsley
11. *Satan* by Gustave Doré
12. *St Sebastian* by Martin Schongauer

This workbook is split into two sections for each Rule. Each section deals with the Rule itself and the arguments brought up by Peterson in each subsection. In the end, there is a section that helps you to consider and analyze your own responses to the material and debates that Jordan Peterson is seeking to expand upon. The final section includes:

- **Goals.** These are three or four sentences that offer a concise overview of the themes brought up in the Rule. They cover the ideas, conclusions, and debates that Jordan Peterson is eager to get across in each section of the book, a useful reference to look at before delving into the chapter summaries above.
- **Activities.** These are questions that are designed to make you reflect on your own responses to the issues that Peterson raises. They are each themed around a particular aspect of the rule and can be used as an opportunity for wider discussion.
- **Checklists.** These are the key takeaways from each Rule, designed to give a snapshot of what is contained in each section.

- **Action plans.** This is for those who want to engage further with the ideas put forward by Peterson. It is a distillation of the advice given by Peterson within each Rule.

Finally, there is a short quiz at the end of the workbook. This is designed to remind the reader of the key ideas and insights offered by Jordan Peterson, and help the reader engage with the core thrust of his arguments and suggestions.

A Note from the Author in the Time of the Pandemic

Jordan B. Peterson begins *Beyond Order* with a very short note that explains that while the need to address the pandemic is important, this book follows his original layout pre-Covid-19.

Overture

This 'Overture', an introduction to *Beyond Order* by Jordan B. Peterson begins by detailing the events in his life on the 5th of February 2020, where he had been hospitalized in Moscow and awoke very confused and agitated. But as he lay there in bed, one of the few things he could remember was the process of writing *Beyond Order* and the difficulties that plagued his family as he wrote.

These difficulties included a near-fatal cancer of his wife Tammy, which impacted Peterson's own mental well-being and he has already suffered from anxiety since 2017. The anxiety and its treatment impacted other areas of his health and he eventually was prescribed benzodiazepine. Following the cessation of his anti-anxiety medication and an increase in the benzodiazepine, he suffered emotional abnormalities and ceased that as well. He was advised to take ketamine as a means to wean himself off of the benzodiazepine and suffered from an awful emotional reaction.

His subsequent withdrawal from benzodiazepine was not a pleasant experience and he continued to suffer from depression and took medication for it. His health continued to deteriorate and he went to a hospital in Toronto. His memory ends there but was told later that the treatment he received was not helpful and he was brought to Moscow by his daughter Mikhaila, and her husband Andrey.

As he convalesced from his akathisia and his subsequent pneumonia picked up in Canada, he had to undergo neurological rehabilitation in Russia. Eventually, he returned to Florida and attempted to wean himself off of the medication he had been given in Russia, and eventually wound up at a Serbian clinic.

He explains that he relates all of this to show that, while the events that befell him and his wife were horrific, he gained some perspective on his work and its importance to his well-being. As a result, *Beyond Order* is unlike his previous book *12 Rules for Life* in that it explores the implications of too much security and control.

He concludes that he hopes this iteration of his thoughts is much wiser and considered than *12 Rules for Life*, and much of this volume is drawn from.

Rule 1: Do Not Carelessly Denigrate Social Institutions or Creative Achievement

Loneliness and Confusion

Jordan B. Peterson begins 'Rule 1' of *Beyond Order* by relaying a little about his experiences with a client who lived in isolation, following a difficult and abusive upbringing. He observed awkward social interactions with the client but found that if he just remained silent for the first fifty minutes of their one-hour sessions, the remaining ten minutes were generally much more relaxed. This example shows communication allows people to organize their minds.

Sanity as a Social Institution

He believes that Freud and Jung did not place enough focus on the role of community on individual mental health. This is why he always looks to see how his clients fit in their environments. He explains that people react to how they are reacted to and adjust their concept of what is normal accordingly. What is more difficult to understand is how social conventions are arrived at in the first place. Values and what is socially acceptable must be negotiated, and when an individual complies with those values, that is when they are deemed 'sane'.

The Point of Pointing

He explains that, in observing his granddaughter, and her love of pointing, pointing, he explains, is similar to the act of naming something—it is identifying an object of note. Words are just an evolved form of points.

What Should We Point to?

Solutions to the issues we face biologically are the most important things we must point to. The complex issues must be reduced to a single point on which we can act, and in so doing all of humanity must be considered.

Bottom Up

These questions of what solutions we must prioritize are based on a deep, neural level of understanding that 'we must survive'. Our human motivational systems are complex but work along the chain of needs from the primal to uniquely human. This hierarchy of needs is often mirrored in social organizations and in the play of infants. These establish what the rules of the game are and who has access to each resource. This is why play is important, and that winning or losing is not scoring a winning goal or preventing one but showing that you are useful to the team.

The Utility of the Fool

Here, Peterson explains how useful it can be to be at the bottom of a hierarchical structure. It is there you have access to the most learning. It is for this reason that the archetypal hero, such as Pinocchio or Harry Potter, can be considered the fool in the opening acts of each story.

The Necessity of Equals

Peterson explains how difficult it can be to move information up or down a hierarchy, which is why communication between peers and friends is so important. It is a key ingredient to the learning of cooperation and social cohesion. He explains how his granddaughter developed her understanding of fair play and sharing through games with her peers. Even as adults, we reduce our predilection for selfishness through teamwork.

Top Dog

People who know how to solve a problem should be given the opportunity to lead, Peterson says. Authority must always be accompanied by ability, otherwise, it is simply wasted power. There must be a distinction made between those ambitious for power over others and those who desire an effective solution to a problem. Those who rise to authority must be willing to open opportunities to those at the bottom and be willing to identify ability in those lower on the hierarchical scale.

Social Institutions Are Necessary - But Insufficient

Here, Peterson explains that social creatures must be predisposed towards maintaining the equilibrium provided by social rules to avoid chaos. However, as circumstances change, there is a need for rules to transform. He explains that our individual ability to adapt to these changes can be dictated by our temperament, whether we have an intrinsic bias towards change or conservatism. Both can fall prey to the extremes of preserving or destroying tradition, unable to distinguish what is useful and what is redundant.

He relates a story in which a distraught young lady came to speak with him about her issues, but that it became a useless conversation to her when it became clear to Peterson that some of her issues stemmed from her politicized morality. Specifically, he mentions that it came from her passion for environmental science and belief in imminent climate-related catastrophe. Peterson found himself dismayed and unable to continue the conversation, nor could he believe that he was able to help given the nature of her complaint.

The Necessity of Balance

Peterson looks at how we naturally follow social conventions because they are often the result of repeated success, and indeed, that the same is true of radical reform. A hierarchical form can make use of both by bringing the two types of people together to transcend their temperaments. The two modes are interdependent, however much they may not wish to admit it.

He admires the imagery of the Genie of the Lamp, and how, like those who seek reform, a genie must be released from constraint from time to time to work his magic. The status quo may be corrupted, and it is only through a creative endeavor that such corruption can be expunged.

Personality as Hierarchy - and Capacity for Transformation

He concludes the chapter with a look at the vital role of stories and storytelling in building personal capacity for balancing respect and the reforming spirit regarding social institutions. Narratives are full of success and tragedy and how our world functions when it comes to the transformation or the maintenance of societal values. Often, the hero is presented as an ideal personality, or as one which is ascending towards the ideal. We draw our narratives and compare them with those of the heroes from personal experience.

He returns to the story of his client who suffered from isolation and how he had to employ a certain creative genius in reconstructing his social life. He needed to develop a new idea of the world around him and began this endeavor by becoming a photographer. At his photography club, he was able to socialize productively and began to develop in other areas too, eventually becoming a commercially successful graphic artist.

He relates how he has seen similar progress in two other clients, both of whom had creative temperaments. So, too, did he see this building of creative appreciation in his granddaughter as she started to socialize.

This idea of narrative and the actions of a hero pointing to a particular rule or a need to break it is well exemplified in the characters in the Harry Potter series. The main characters often exemplify how one might both follow the rules and break them when they become redundant.

His granddaughter, soon after learning how to point, learned more complex ideas about narratives, insisting on being called Pocahontas after her favorite Disney character and doll. She was able to understand and identify with the doll and the character and her own desire to emulate its characteristics.

In much the same way, people have, for a millennium, discovered characters who they wish to emulate and imitate. Here he provides the example of Jesus, as both a follower of tradition and a breaker of it. He was, as Peterson invites us in this whole chapter, one who did not denigrate social institutions or acts of creative success with undue care.

Goal:

In this first rule, Peterson exhorts us to be considered in our approach to both institutions and those which would subvert them with a certain amount of caution. The rule reflects the dual temperament of modern society, those who seek to conserve traditions and those who seek to remove them. Both have a place in hierarchical structures, Peterson explains, and one cannot survive without the other. But both also have extremes which may be gone to which will render useful innovations, whether past or future, into dust. Something which we will all be the poorer for.

Lesson:

Activity 1:
Peterson makes points about traditions, societal values, and social conventions in this chapter. His argument is that while there are always conventions that must abide by, we should not discount the act of innovation in order to retain them. For this activity, write out a list of social conventions that you believe have become obsolete that maintain their hold over the general public.

Activity 2:
Conversely, Peterson also makes a point about traditional values that have retained their usefulness, simply by virtue of their effectiveness. What societal values continue to benefit people as a whole that you would not like to see done away with?

Checklist:

Key takeaways from this chapter are:
- Society and its intricate hierarchy inform what is sane in the individual.

- Words are indicators of that which has value to the individual.
- Hierarchy is a natural pattern.
- Every level of hierarchy has its use.
- Authority must be accompanied by capability.
- Progression and Conservation are both necessary and must keep each other in check.

Action Plan:

- Interrogate and internalize which societal values are necessary to be considered sane.
- Discover where you sit in terms of the various hierarchies you are part of and embrace what you can of them.
- When questioning authority, ask yourself whether those you question are there through ability or through tyranny.
- Be comfortable with the idea that both liberal and conservative temperaments must co-exist and will each have their use.
- Consider how important the creative function is when it comes to building your own narrative.

Rule 2: Imagine Who You Could Be, and Then Aim Single-Mindedly at That

Who Are You - and Who Could You Be?

Jordan Peterson begins this next rule of *Beyond Order* by asking us how we know who we are, and what else could we be given our potential. He explains that Socrates believed that learning is simply a form of remembering, and to some extent, Peterson agrees. It is how we determine who we are and what we could become.

The Emergence of the Unforgettable

With the understanding that learning is an act of remembering, it is worthwhile looking at what becomes unforgettable. Stories are often distillations of observed behaviors and experiences that strike us emotionally. Unforgettable stories—he uses the example of the Israelites flight from Egypt—are those which elicit a universal response and motivate our attention.

Materia Prima: Who You Could Be (1)

In this section, he first draws our attention to the woodcut which opens the chapter. It depicts archaic symbols of dragons, the male and female element as well as astral bodies like the sun, the moon, and astrological symbols. The image is known as the Materia Prima, or the primal element, something from which medieval and early modern alchemists believed all matter was derived. Peterson uses this idea as an analogy for how we might consider the information with which we build our own personalities. How we interpret that information can inform how we build our world-view, as we might when reading the contents of a letter.

He draws attention, next, to the image of a winged sphere, popularly described by J K Rowling in her Harry Potter series as a quidditch ball, but actually an archaic symbol for chaos. It is associated with the winged god Mercury, the messenger of the gods, often the bringer of fortune, and, as in Harry Potter, an invitation to the game. It is a reminder, Peterson tells us, that even under the most strenuous circumstances we must learn to play fair

Next, he draws attention to the dragon in the woodcut, a monster of immense danger but the archetype of a guardian of treasure. This can symbolize, in alchemical terms, the dangerous but coveted knowledge of the immortals.

Finally, we have the image of the two-headed god, Rebis, the androgynous male and female element of a fully formed personality. This symbolizes triumph over adversity.

Polytheism into Monotheism, and the Emergence of the Virtuous Hero: Who You Could Be (II)

Peterson now looks at one of the oldest hero myths in the world, that of the story of goddess Tiamat and god Apsu as the parents of the elder Babylonian gods. In order to engage with this story, we must understand that ancient texts like this one personify elemental reality—thus does Tiamat, the element of saltwater, enter into sexual union with Apsu, the element of freshwater. He goes on to relate the myth in detail, which comes to its climax when the strongest of the elder gods, Marduk, defeats Tiamat, his grandmother, to become all-powerful. Peterson tells this is the embodiment of how polytheism became monotheism.

He follows this with an exposition of the similar stories of St George and the Dragon, St Patrick and St Michael, and the modern stories of *The Hobbit* and even *Iron Man*. All of these stories make us of the idea that one hero rises out of chaos to battle the forces of darkness.

Hero, Dragon, Death, and Rebirth: Who You Could Be (III)

He begins this section with an interrogation of *Harry Potter and the Chamber of Secrets*, specifically the hero narrative within. Harry, who is orphaned as many heroes in western literature are, must rise up against a malevolent force that is preying on his schoolmates. Here, we once again see the reptilian terror, this time in the form of the snake, rise up to be cast as an eternal enemy. In many respects, the story in this volume of the *Harry Potter* series is very similar to the myth of Beowulf and similar also to the blockbuster *Jaws*.

In each of these tales, the terror of the deep guards a hidden treasure. As in *The Hobbit* Harry has to embrace the dark side of himself in order to achieve his goal. While we might, as the most primal part of our brain tells us to, freeze in the face of terror and survive, so too will the terror itself. In these stories, the hero overcomes his instinctual fear to overcome the terror and destroy it, making the world a safer place for society.

Finally, Harry is bitten in the final fight with the Basilisk of the story and is only revived through the tears of the phoenix. It is a classic tale of rebirth, which owes much to the constant reiteration of the hero myth.

How to Act

When considering how we might put these hero narratives into action in our own lives we might look first at the moments of chaos in our lives and see how we might embolden ourselves to act rather than freeze in fear. We rely on these structures and narratives, however deluded it may be, to motivate ourselves towards action for good or ill.

As with the Christian narrative, we must be prepared for figurative rebirth in order to overcome predatory evil. As we as everyday people cannot very well go attacking snakes and large lizards, we must be aiming for something that we can conceptualize in our own lives and allow our most lofty and noble ideals to encourage us to drive towards it. It may not be a story out of fantasy books but it is an adventure nonetheless.

Goal:

In this second rule of Jordan Peterson's book *Beyond Order,* he seeks to elaborate on the narratives we have consumed since time immemorial and investigate how we have assimilated them into our personalities. He looks at the mystical imagery of alchemy and how it may apply to hero myths and the famous 'Overcoming the Monster' narratives that populate almost the entirety of ancient and modern literature and culture. He urges us to embrace these fantastic narratives as a means to pushing ourselves towards grander personal narratives. In a sense, it is a call to embrace our creative selves.

Lesson:

Activity 1:
This chapter is very much about the inescapable personal narratives we all consume and identify with about ourselves. In the most open and honest way you can, write about a personal, defining moment in which chaos has called you to action.

Activity 2:
The second section of the woodcut, which begins this chapter, depicts a great and fiery dragon, a monster that guards the key to hidden treasure. In your personal narrative, what figurative monster do you feel you need to overcome in order to gain the treasure, which will unlock the best in you?

Activity 3:
The last section of the woodcut depicts an androgynous human figure, the purest elements of masculinity and femininity. Peterson urges us to embrace these aspects to build towards our rebirth as a hero. What are the qualities you would expect to see in yourself if you could be reborn as your best self?

Checklist:
Key takeaways from this chapter are: • We are hardwired to consume and identify narratives in order to build our social persona. • In order to attain the best of ourselves, we must - at times - sacrifice the part of ourselves that blindly clutches at self-preservation. • Hero narratives have long sought to present to humanity the very best of our personal ideals as something to aspire to. • Whatever our backgrounds or personal circumstances, there is always room for lofty idealism as a means to bringing ourselves closer to the hero inside ourselves.

Action Plan:
• Embrace certain aspects of your darkest self in order to push yourself towards noble intentions. • Embrace hero narratives as a means to understanding your personal ideals and what you consider 'fair play.' • Consider chaos as a call to rise up and meet the challenge it presents. • Read widely and deeply to understand how hero narratives have built the global narrative canon.

Rule 3: Do Not Hide Unwanted Things in the Fog

Those Damned Plates

Jordan Peterson begins this third rule of *Beyond Order* with an anecdote about his father-in-law Dell, a man who seems to be very content and laid back, not to mention in good health for a man of eighty-eight. He is a man who does what he does without complaining, even when Peterson's late mother-in-law, Beth, developed dementia. However, on one occasion, Dell lost his temper, specifically about having to eat off of small plates. While the story is somewhat amusing, Peterson reflects that it may well be that there were underlying issues that Dell had hidden and only vented because of the plate.

Just Not Worth the Fight

Peterson now relates a story of one of his clients who came to see him, ostensibly about a problem with her career. However, as each session progressed it became more and more apparent that her issues were not with her career - she moved jobs without any issues - but with her marriage. She had little control over her own surroundings at home and her husband was overbearing and obsessed with 1970s pop art, which the whole apartment was covered with. Ultimately, it meant that she felt like a stranger in her own home.

We may be tempted to leave matters like this, seemingly trivial on the surface, and move on. But they have a way of coming back to us if left unaddressed and sometimes in larger, more damaging forms.

Corruption: Commission and Omission

Here, Peterson looks at the idea of deception and self-deception as a means of corruption. He explains that it is possible - and he has experience of it - to believe two entirely paradoxical ideas at the same time. He turns to Freud as someone who pioneered the exploration of self-deception as a function of mental illness that paradox is intrinsic to the difficulties caused by competing forces of the human psyche.

But Freud did not factor in the failure to do something good—a 'sin of omission'—as another contribution to mental illness. In those who suffer from trauma, it might manifest as a guilt-complex. Elsewhere it may manifest as a criminal activity such as 'turning a blind eye' to illegal activity.

Freud also did not examine the possibility that things that we experience are not necessarily understood. Peterson reminds us that we look at the world from a basic point of view at first glance and only process complex information later on. We do not always have the opportunity to avoid self-deception and often end up working off of only half processed information.

What is the Fog?
He begins to illustrate how fear and anxiety contribute to a figurative fog that may keep us from truly understanding the issues that beset us. Fear is an important driver for keeping us from true knowledge and true understanding of our challenges, simply because of a natural sense of self-preservation, a case of 'what you don't know can't hurt you.'

We might even thrive despite the thought there are unaddressed issues at play, that may well manifest themselves as mood swings or deeper health issues. They might keep us from pursuing certain goals out of what seems to be unexplainable anxiety.

We are often terrified of failure, but in order to make progress towards our personal goals, we must accept it as an inevitability. We must admit to our most difficult emotions and even past trauma if we are to dispel the fog.

Events and Memories

Peterson begins this last section by looking out how our memories are not bound by chronology, and often organize themselves in clandestine ways that we do not always understand. They can be modified and refined—and occasionally corrupted.

In order to discover useful information in our experiences, we must be prepared to do some hard digging. We may discover ugly things that we shrink from at times, and occasionally insights that suddenly bear up and shine a light on corners of our mind we didn't know existed. Peterson urges us to avoid attempting to discard memories or keep them shut away, as they have a tendency to spill out into other things and influence us in ways we might not be fully conscious of. We must see memory as an opportunity to keep the fog away forever.

Goal:

In this chapter of *Beyond Order* Jordan Peterson draws on his expertise as a psychologist to look at the dangers of repressed trauma and repetitive, destructive behavior. His focus begins on the trivialities of life - the petty squabbles, the ignored phone calls, etc. - and provides examples of where these small acts of irritation can amount to psychological issues later on. He looks broadly at the motives we might have for leaving things unaddressed and the dire consequences that may stem from the avoidance of oppressive events and memories.

Lesson:

As with any mental health issue or personal difficulty, it is advisable to seek professional help where you can before attempting to access painful memories. For our purposes, it may be useful to look at friends or colleagues to maintain an objective distance.

Activity 1:
Think of someone you know who exhibits neurotic or eccentric behavior. What things do they typically, if at all, lose their temper over?

Activity 2:
With the same person, how often do you see them back down from a challenge and what kind of challenges do they face regularly?

Activity 3:
Using these two questions, what would you say is the cause of their particular 'fog'? What fears and anxieties are keeping them from their true potential?

Checklist:
Key takeaways from this chapter are: • Losing one's temper over little things are often a symptom of something much larger • We focus our attention on trivialities to keep us from addressing the more overbearing challenges. • Often, what might seem like a traumatizing event may have been a case of self-deception, either through commission, or intentional or unintentional omission. • If we allow our fears and anxieties to take control of our memories and how we process events we risk damaging or neurotic behavior.

Action Plan:
• Access and analyze your memories regularly. • Address the trivialities in your life as though they were the most important issues you face. • Whilst we may have difficult or traumatic memories locked away, we may also have insights or new information on those memories that will take the sting out of them.

Rule 4: Notice that Opportunity Lurks Where Responsibility has Been Abdicated

Make Yourself Invaluable

Jordan Peterson begins this section of *Beyond Order* by looking at some of the issues his clients have brought to him in their professional lives. Often, there are those in the workplace who are incompetent or unsuited to their jobs at best, or bullying and narcissistic at worst. It is here that, for those who see these poor behaviors on display, there are opportunities to be taken. We must be bold when these opportunities occur and volunteer ourselves for the work, regardless of how daunting it may seem.

Responsibility and Meaning

He continues by looking at the notion that 'life is suffering' as is often found in eastern religions as well as literature. In fact, he goes on to look in detail at the story of *Peter Pan*, a boy who refuses to grow up in contrast with his female counterpart Wendy, who chooses the adult life over the playground that is Neverland.

Our responsibility, as is suggested by all religious texts, is to accept suffering and difficulty as an intrinsic part of life. It is only through suffering that we might unlock our true potential and expose the hidden forces that dwell within us. In the language of the hero myth, it is only the trial that can reveal to us the 'magic words', as Peterson puts it, that will open the inner sanctum and lead us to the treasure we seek.

Rescue Your Father: Osiris and Horus

Peterson now continues by outlining the Egyptian myth of Osiris and Horus. Osiris was worshipped as the founding god of Egypt, but as he aged, he grew 'willfully blind', and closed his eyes against his kingdom.

But Osiris had a rival, his brother Set. Osiris's willful blindness gave Set an opportunity to seize Osiris and dismember him - though as an immortal, Osiris is not dead. In fact, one vital member of him is found by the goddess Isis, who impregnates herself following her discovery and returns to the Underworld to give birth to Horus. It is he who returns to confront Set and has one of his eyes torn out in the battle but emerges victorious. He recovers his eye and banishes Set.

Peterson explains that in the Egyptian pantheon, Horus was but an incarnation of Osiris. Likewise, he suggests that as we move through our own narrative, we might consider that we might also be an avatar of previous heroic figures. We too might be heroes who plunge into cavernous and challenging depths to redeem our fathers and take on the mantle of our ancestors.

And Who Might That Be?

Peterson talks now to the most selfish part of ourselves, that which seeks only self-preservation and self-care. He says that often, among those who exhibit such tendencies, there is a difficulty in distinguishing what it is that we must preserve and take care of, whether our present selves or our future selves.

Sensible people will look as far into the future as they can reasonably predict to preserve themselves, and thus will necessarily take on responsibility for themselves. We must make peace with our future selves and begin to take care of that person in the present.

Happiness and Responsibility

In the pursuit of happiness, Peterson says, we often forget the future. Happiness is, unfortunately, a present emotion and is not a commodity that is easily stored for later use. We must instead seek to harness the motivation to act responsibly and reliably.

He challenges the notion that happiness comes from attainment, for when something is attained, there is always some further goal drawing us along, so that our attainments never quite seem as mountainous as we would like to have imagined. Instead, he suggests that we concentrate on larger goals, those of acting decently with our fellows, which, while broad in their scope, are more likely to bring contentment than short-term impulses.

Pick up the Extra Weight

Peterson concludes the chapter with a reflection on our pursuit for meaning rather than happiness. He explains that meaning is only derived from the levels of responsibility we are prepared to shoulder. He relates the biblical story of Abraham, who, having spent many idle years at his father's house is called forth by Yahweh to his destiny. It is clear from the moment he begins his journey that this will not be an easy task, but it will be a meaningful adventure that will set him up as the father of a dynasty.

Such responsibilities and consequent deeper understanding of life, he concludes, are worth more than transitory happiness.

Goal:

Jordan Peterson uses this chapter of *Beyond Order* to investigate the notion of responsibility in all its forms. He starts by looking at the responsibilities in our professional lives but very quickly moves on to the more philosophical attitudes and outcomes of taking on responsibility. He is eager to caution us against the idle pursuit of happiness and instead urges us to embrace suffering as a means to live a more fulfilling life, full of meaning and understanding.

Lesson:

Activity 1:
Peterson explains that often we do not take responsibility or respond to a call to action through fear of failure. Take a look at your career or education thus far and write out a list of times where you could have taken responsibility for a project or initiative that no one else was prepared to undertake. Reflect on why you didn't take the opportunity.

Activity 2:
Discuss, with your friends or colleagues, events or memories which, while not exactly happy, are fulfilling and meaningful memories nonetheless. What is the common denominator in these meaningful memories?

Checklist:

Key takeaways from this chapter are:
- We have a responsibility to ourselves and others to accept challenges
- Our responsibility to ourselves is not just to ourselves in the present but in the future as well.
- Happiness is a transitory emotion, but the meaning is long

lasting and ultimately more rewarding.

- In accepting our own responsibilities, we may provide opportunities for others to accept their own.

Action Plan:

- Whenever you see responsibility being discarded, take the initiative and shoulder it yourself.
- Make plans for the future that allow you to grow in understanding, not just in attainment.
- Make an investigation of your family and friends, past and present, and consider what responsibilities you have for them.

Rule 5: Do Not Do What You Hate

Pathological Order in its Day-to-Day Guise

Jordan Peterson starts this section of *Beyond Order* by relating how one particular client of his had to deal with some workplace discussion over whether the use of the term 'flip chart' was derogatory to Filipinos. Peterson goes on to list other examples where terms and words have been questioned as appropriate for use in the public sphere and explains that this is a dangerous path to the wholesale and ludicrous omission of terms that are not deemed 'politically correct'.

He moves on to the theory that there are 'learning styles', namely the auditory, verbal, physical and logical, and so forth. He explains that there is no evidence for adopting learning styles as a means of improving performance, though students may prefer one style over another, nor evidence that teachers can assess each students learning style. When one of his clients challenged it publicly, she had to face the fear of reprisal professionally, but having done so, Peterson tells us that she found a great amount of fulfillment.

He explains that it is through such small acts of defiance against the common order that we can be sure we are leading a 'moral and careful' life, to ensure that such things as 'learning styles' and challenging terminology do not lead down the slippery slope to totalitarianism.

Fortify Your Position

Here, Peterson looks at how culture descends into chaos when people do not stand up for it against idealists who seek to subvert it. For this, we must not do the things we hate and challenge the attitudes and behaviors we see that are removing freedom of expression. He goes on to recognize that often we might feel like we are only a small piece of the puzzle, but it is only by standing up among others that change or conservation can happen.

Practicalities

In our day-to-day lives, Peterson says we might look at our workplaces and see whether there might be better options that will have us at our ease with our conscience if the culture is something with which we do not agree. He explains that we can either confront the behaviors we see displayed or move on. Though he recognizes that the rejection rate for new jobs is very high, it is not personal - but of course, leaving the workplace culture that suffocates and controls you might well be worth the risk.

However, he does give one small caveat that we must be in a position that we can gain employment elsewhere. Though you should remain certain that you are leaving the workplace culture that is causing you such issues, you should ensure you are leaving with all the skills and training you might need to find work. He finishes the chapter by making it clear that he does not mean resentment as a call to leave your workplace, but that it must only come from a call of your conscience.

Goal:

Jordan Peterson uses this section of *Beyond Order* to look at how we might often encounter issues in our professional lives, which call for us to be bold about those issues that we hold dear. He lists a few examples of absurd ideologically motivated workplace initiatives which have stifled freedom of expression and how it has been imperative for those clients who have relayed them to challenge them in order to maintain a clear conscience. He tells us that we must not put up with it, nor acquiesce to these emerging societal institutions if they plague our conscience.

Lesson:

Activity 1:
Peterson lists a few examples of issues that have faced his clients at their respective workplaces. Among these, he lists the radical management of terminology, the adoption of unscientific ideas, or what he terms 'totalitarian utopianism'. Make a list of things that you would rather not see, in an ideal world, in your current place of work.

Activity 2:
Again, considering your workplace culture, if you know of a particular idea or initiative that you object to on a moral basis, see if you can engage in a conversation about it with a trusted colleague and discuss the ramifications of such an initiative.

Activity 3:
Peterson explains that, for those who have the appropriate skills and support, it is wise to look for a better workplace setting if that which you are working in already is culturally predisposed to causing you moral discomfort. With this in mind, consider what your ideal workplace would look like.

Checklist:
Key takeaways from this chapter are: • We have a responsibility to our conscience to act in accordance with it. • Ideologies and behaviors with which we do not agree on a moral basis must be challenged. • We must remove ourselves from stifling or culturally dogmatic workplaces or career scenarios. • If we cannot remove ourselves efficiently, we should develop towards a position in which we can.

Action Plan:
• Assess your workplace for issues that you find difficult to agree with or that you feel need to be addressed. • Be sure of your position and defend it articulately and with a thorough understanding. • Remove yourself or challenge situations in which you feel uncomfortable on a moral basis.

Rule 6: Abandon Ideology

The Wrong Places

Jordan Peterson begins this section of *Beyond Order* by looking at the success of his last book and wonders how it managed to strike a chord with so many people. He explains how a previously homeless man had read the book, was able to turn his life around, and met him after one particular talk. Peterson often hears stories like this and believes that his talks across the English-speaking world gave him a great opportunity to observe the zeitgeist.

He explains that in many instances if he spoke about responsibility, it was often met with silence. It is not an easy sell, he admits, and as a consequence, our attitude to responsibility as adults has suffered in an era where parents are afraid to encourage their children to embrace it.

Perhaps He Is Only Sleeping

This part of Rule 6 begins with an interrogation of the famous Nietzsche declaration that 'God is dead.' Peterson explains that this was a reflection of Nietzsche's fear that Judeo-Christian values were being subjected to criticism and that the central part of them was being challenged—which might have dire consequences for order.

Peterson explains that Nietzsche's fear was that we might lose ourselves to nihilism in the absence of a monotheistic structure. Both he and Dostoevsky, Peterson says, foresaw the rise of communism. These were not the socialist-lite movements of Britain, Scandinavia, and Canada, which had working-class improvement as a central tenet of their dogma, as Peterson terms it, but the collectivism of Russia and China.

But these fears of Nietzsche and Dostoevsky about nihilism were unfounded, and it took Freud and Jung to demonstrate that we do not possess the genius to build ideologies out of nothing. And yet there remain certain individual and collective experiences that we have that one might call 'religious' without the backdrop of the religion itself. Indeed, some movements of the twentieth century that have tried to build entirely new ideologies have failed catastrophically and with painful consequences for everyone.

The Fatal Attraction of the False Idol
Peterson now looks at ideologies that he perceives as 'false idols' namely conservatism, feminism, and environmentalism, amongst other terms. He explains that these are forms of religion that follow one specific set of beliefs rather than proven ideas. He explains that the process by which these systems are generated often come from well-meaning ideologues who look for solutions to problems such as poverty and oppression. There can be no single solution to these issues, and all require careful analysis rather than a wholesale answer which casts villains and heroes.

Those who engage in ideological reductions are dangerous and are the intellectual form of fundamentalists, Peterson says. When we encounter such rigid and unyielding reductionist narratives we must be wary and analyze their beliefs carefully, looking beyond their pseudointellectual posturing and attempt to discover what informs them.

Resentment
Peterson concludes the chapter by looking at the ideological pursuit of victimhood as a means of claiming absolute innocence. It informs much public discourse and often does more

harm than good. Those claiming oppression might feel they have *cart blanche* to become the oppressors themselves.

It can lead to the persecution of individuals of a certain demographic, simply because they belong to that demographic and leads only to further division. An ideology that allows this to happen inevitably leads to more extreme ideologies until there can be no meaningful discourse.

Goal:

This section of *Beyond Order* has Peterson looking at the dangers of becoming entrenched with ideology. He looks back at the development of ideology since the end of the 19th century and a few of the destructive ideas that have stemmed from an ideology that focuses on one-solution narratives rather than nuanced rational debate. He explains that certain ideologies have replaced religious fundamentalism and can be every bit as dangerous, as can be seen in the communist, fascist and ultra-conservative movements which have wreaked untold havoc across the world over the twentieth century.

Lesson:

Activity 1:
This chapter looks at the dangers of ideology. Think carefully about the definition of ideology and write out a list of features of any particular ideology you believe identifies it as particularly dangerous. This can be its history, the extreme events it may have led to, or the way it has shaped discourse following its emergence.

Activity 2:
Peterson also looks at the idea that we cannot build ideologies out of nothing. If you subscribe to an ideology or hold particular personal beliefs, make a list of previous ideologies from which they may have taken their roots.

Checklist:

Key takeaways from this chapter are:
- There are no ideologies that have not been drawn from previous ideologies.
- We must accept responsibility for our own behavior and not

look to ideology or religions to provide cover for them.
- Those who claim superior knowledge through ideology and blindly offer sweeping solutions to society's great ills are to be treated carefully.
- Victimhood does not guarantee all-pervading innocence.

Action Plan:

- Treat ideologues with caution
- Accept responsibility for your actions and words
- If you are subjected to persecution or abuse, do not assume it absolves you of responsibility to treat others with respect.

Rule 7: Work as Hard as You Possibly Can On at Least One Thing and See What Happens

The Value of Heat and Pressure

This section of *Beyond Power* begins with Jordan Peterson explaining how diamonds are formed following intense heat and pressure. Similarly, intense forces that act upon a person may be said to follow the same process. It is only through intense pressure that we might be transformed into the most beautiful iteration of ourselves. He explains that what happens in these pressurized situations, like the diamond, all our qualities are brought together in an internal union which makes us both resilient and maximizes our potential to shine.

The Worst Decision of All

Peterson continues by relating how when he was studying for his Ph.D., he noticed that those who continued in more difficult programs after their initial programs displayed a marked improvement in personal interactions and sense of direction. This observation was made manifest in his patients later on, and what became clear is that mental health improves when the individual is regularly challenged.

For those who do not make the decision to undertake these regular challenges, it is very easy to drift and, further down the line, lose any idea of who they really are.

Discipline and Unity

He goes on to look at how the psychology of those who are able to make the decision on what they should be doing for the rest of their lives develops. Often it starts with an early predilection for self-organization and self-discipline, where good parents are keen to allow the child to complete a task or process by themselves.

Further along, the child must learn how to co-operate and organize alongside their peers. This should be reinforced with parental emphasis on self-discipline and orderly behavior. The social world will allow the child to pull together the multiple facets of his personality into union so that he can play and work with his teammates without disruption.

As the child grows into an adult, he may become an apprentice of sorts and learn how to work with the parameters of a structure. With enough personal discipline and adherence to the social tenets of his sphere, he will eventually become the master of his future.

Dogma and Spirit

Jordan Peterson concludes the chapter by looking at the useful qualities of rules of limitation, the 'Thou Shalt Nots'. As an example, he lists the biblical Ten Commandments and suggests these were, in fact, the rules to maintain a stable society. Their central idea, the theme, is that those following the commandments must subjugate themselves to them in order to partake of the Israelite society.

He explains that western society is underpinned by these Judeo-Christian values, whether consciously or not, and is embodied by figures like Christ, who, while revolutionary during the gospels, also maintains certain aspects of the pre-established order of the Jewish faith.

Likewise, as we work towards our purpose, we are also raising ourselves above the clamoring masses and will have the opportunity to revolutionize our own industries or groups.

Goal:

This chapter of *Beyond Order* by Jordan Peterson looks specifically at the role of self-discipline and personal challenges in the formation of purpose and personality. He explains that continued and intensive challenges and honing of skills produce fine work and social habits that make one a highly efficient, useful member of society. This begins at an early age, and parents should be encouraged to ensure their children strive to complete tasks by themselves, developing much desired self-organizational skills in the process.

Lesson:

Activity 1:
Think of the last time you achieved something major by yourself, whether it is a personal project, work task, or educational assignment. Write down what self-disciplinary methods you used to achieve that task.

Activity 2:
Think, now, of the last time you completed a group project. Consider, discuss or debrief with those involved the key moments that allowed your group to thrive. How many of those moments involved self-discipline on your part? How many usually forthright or lively members of the group became compliant to the group needs as opposed to their individual needs?

Checklist:

Key takeaways from this chapter are:
- Self-discipline is often learned early in life.
- Unity within a group is often a good way of building self-discipline.

- Working towards a purpose inevitably leads to greater sense of purpose.
- Social skills are built through exposure to parameters.

Action Plan:

- If you are not one who is generally self-disciplined, look for opportunities to challenge your attention skills or any bad habits you may have fallen into.
- Undertake as many group activities as you can in order to build self-discipline when it comes to adherence to the rules of that group.
- Follow any sense of purpose that you have to its logical conclusion - you never what opportunities it may lead to.
- Embrace the idea of parameters - they are the pressure that is required for you to crystalize your purpose.

Rule 8: Try to Make One Room in Your Home as Beautiful as Possible

Cleaning Your Room is Not Enough

Jordan Peterson reiterates, in this part of *Beyond Order*, the call for people to be tidying up their rooms which was well disseminated from his previous book. He explains that he has found it a personal challenge since he published the piece of advice, and understands that it is not always such a simple task as it first appears.

But further than that, he explains that a room should reflect the beauty and majesty of culture, whether it is literary culture, art, or music. He explains that art is an important conduit for our transcendent selves, and it is of great benefit to us to connect with that part of ourselves regularly.

Memory and Vision

He reflects on how well, as a child, he knew all the areas and designs of his surroundings. As we get older, our ability to engage with our surroundings lessens and we become alienated from our space.

While it may mean that we are more pragmatic in many ways, it leaves us void of some of the richness of our environment. It's something which is of import to all the great poets (here he quotes Wordsworth at length). For such poets, the landscape, our habitat, and our immediate surroundings are all linked with the past, present, and future.

So, too, do artists such as Van Gogh see the world as an interconnected paradise of perception, of which we, as viewers, are only given the most cursory of glances? He suggests that such things have a tendency to be isolated from the general public, and many of us forget to engage with these visions of wonder. In short, we have lost track of that childlike sense of wonder.

The Land You Know, the Land You Do Not Know, and the Land You Cannot Even Imagine

Here, Peterson looks at the realms of internal vision. In particular, he looks at the archetypal landscape, which is made up of that which is commonplace to us, that which is commonplace to others, and that which is uncommon. He explains that it is possible to begin to build a picture of that which is uncommon by reacting physically to something which might startle us or otherwise seem alien within our commonplace landscape.

Artists, he explains, are those people who can see the alien in a landscape or habitat and assimilate it quickly into the commonplace. They transform chaos into order, without ever entirely realizing what they are doing—a key factor in expression.

For Peterson, viewing a work of art is a quasi-religious experience, an expression of the divine. Works of art are sites of pilgrimage, even for those who profess atheism, and the awe they inspire is nothing less than sacred.

One Room

Peterson now relates how he and his wife spent a lot of time beautifying their living room. He details some of the pieces which adorn the walls, including Soviet paintings, Native South American derived art, and church architecture. Many of his pieces he discovered on eBay, and he has a taste, specifically, for

Russian landscape painting. Often these are propaganda pieces from the Soviet era, but he explains that it is interesting to him to note how well the art shines through despite the purpose.

He later relates a story about how he had asked a senior administrator about redecorating an office with industrial grey paint called Hammerite and was surprised when she said no. He laments that she resisted his entreaty because it would have been something everyone would have wanted to do. Eventually, he gathered himself and worked with an artist and the administration of the university to create an office that had a 'dropped copper ceiling'. He explains that it is now of particular note to the potential new hires.

After questioning why he met with such resistance, he relates the issue that often faces Wildebeest, in that lions often attack those which are easily identifiable. In summary, because he chose to be different, he was taking an artistic risk.

Not Decoration

He concludes by explaining some of the finer points of modern art. Many people shun the grotesque or abstract forms of modern art, and though Peterson has an appreciation for fine art and beautiful painting, he believes that art is exploration, rather than decoration. Anything which stokes an unfamiliar or exhilarating response can be considered artistic, and we should allow ourselves to experience such things as they occur.

Goal:

Here, Jordan Peterson expands on his previous exhortation that we must keep our spaces clutter-free. Our responses to art are often formed by our appreciation for wonder as children. He admits that he has found it difficult himself over the previous few years since his life became a lot busier, but he uses it as a platform to take a look at the importance of art in our lives. He explains that art is a window into the greater part of the human spirit. He goes on to explain his own understanding and attitude towards personal decor and how he has set up the artwork in his living room. Further, he takes the opportunity to explain how art can be beyond what is aesthetically beautiful.

Lesson:

Activity 1:
Peterson begins the chapter by extolling us to find room in our lives for beauty and what we value most in terms of art and aesthetics. Spend a little time, as Peterson has done, taking a look through the online collections of the greatest art museums in the world, making careful notes of what art you respond to best.

Activity 2:
Having now begun to understand what forms and movements of artwork you appreciate, take a little time to work out how you might beautify your room.

Activity 3:
In addition to the above activities, make a list of memories involving places of dramatic and compelling visual impact - not necessarily beauty - and look to see whether you can find art that reflects that, no matter how you respond.

Checklist:

Key takeaways from this chapter are:
- Art is a window into transcendence.
- As children, we have a closer connection to the sense of wonder that can reside in the everyday.
- Artists and poets are people who have retained that childlike ability to view the wondrous aspects of their surroundings.
- It is imperative to pursue the artistic urge, regardless of personal taste.
- Not all art must soothe, it can also challenge.

Action Plan:

- Find your particular form of art.
- Reflect on your memories of place and form as children.
- Fill your room with inspiring artwork and objects.
- Keep your room clutter-free.
- Allow yourself to be challenged by art.

Rule 9: If Old Memories Still Upset You, Write Them Down Carefully and Completely

But is Yesterday Finished with You?

Jordan Peterson begins this section of *Beyond Order* by looking at the consequences of poor behavior. We might have wronged people and are, rightly, shunned by them and perhaps now feel remorse - that is, a desire to not replicate the wrong we have done.

Peterson explains that at times, we recall these painful memories or painful memories, in general, we have done without any agency on our part. We do not wish to recall them, but they arrive anyway. It is important that we make an effort to recall these memories accurately, however, in order to analyze what lessons might still be drawn from them.

Do Not Fall Twice into the Same Pit

In this short section, Peterson relates how one of his clients had suffered horrific sexual abuse as a child - but expresses his horror and surprise when she related that the abuser was only two years older than she was. He relates how he approached the patient by expressing what he had imagined the scenario to have been like, but that the offending child was no more than six, and that he did not fit how one might imagine sexual abuse as an adult - rather kids that they poorly supervised kids were playing doctor. Though of course, Peterson is keen to emphasize that for the patient this memory was still current, as those who suffer trauma often experience trauma.

He admits that the case left him in a philosophical quandary, as to what the reality of the situation was. Is it the memory we build as children or the context we add to it as adults?

Possessed by Ghosts

Next, he recalls another client whose memory was clouded, likely by a traumatic event. In one session, the client related how his family believed he was possessed and he was inclined to agree. He was subject to occasional seizures, and Peterson soon ascertained that these might well have been episodes of sleep paralysis, a condition which has, historically, been associated with night terrors and terrifying hallucinations.

Peterson also learned that the client's previous relationship and how it had ended with the client being assaulted. In addition, the family that the client came from was deeply religious and superstitious, with very unusual beliefs. He was eventually diagnosed with a form of somatization disorder. He relates how Peterson tried out a form of hypnotherapy on the client, to which the client retold his story about being assaulted by his boyfriend. This was followed by another round of hypnotherapy and the client soon stopped having convulsions.

Uncomprehended Malevolence

In this section, Peterson recounts another client who had been a victim of bullying and was on antipsychotic medication. In these sessions, Peterson asked the client to break each life event into structural elements and talk and write about the experiences. With Peterson's help, he recounted every section of his life in fluid detail, including the revelation that the bullying started when he refused a date with a girl.

Potential Into Actuality

Peterson explains that people often adopt concerns about things that might happen. This often leads to winding and complex investigations into the potential scenarios in the future and can halt the decision-making process. Often these scenarios are built from preconceived ideas drawn from painful memories.

Decision-making is hard at the best of times, but we must learn to understand how big an impact our agency has. Without the ability to make appropriate decisions, we are regarded as lacking in integrity and it becomes difficult to build positive relationships. This will mean that our memories will once again exert a hold on our lives.

The Word as Savior

This chapter concludes with a reflection that we are all active in the building of a world. We are guided by stories, both ours and those of other people. He explores the book of Genesis and the ways in which the story of creation is told, specifically the importance of 'the Word.'

Like the biblical God, it is our responsibility to create order out of chaos where we find it, and this extends to our past. In the act of organizing our memories through careful writing and interrogating, we are ordering what might otherwise seem a mess in our lives.

Jordan Peterson is keen to have us spend time investigating our personal stories with an objective and analytical eye in this section of *Beyond Order*. It gives us the opportunity to revisit painful memories with new information and context, also to draw out some of the poison in the process. It can also afford us the opportunity to move past issues which may hold us back from appropriate decision-making. Ultimately, it allows us to create some semblance of order in our lives.

Lesson:

Activity 1:
Take a moment to think of any memory, preferably one that you don't revisit often either a favorite or one that you find particularly compelling for whatever reason. Think about how the imagery is mapped out, what scents might be involved, or sounds you might remember. When you have a clear image in your head, write down as much of the layout - not the event - as possible.

Either
Activity 2(a):
Go to (or investigate through the internet if necessary using image search engines) the area involved. Get as full an image as possible of the area as you can.

Or
Activity 2 (b):
If this is a shared memory with someone you are still in contact with, see if you can discuss how you view the area and the senses.

Activity 3:
Revisit your initial description. How accurate is it now that you

have a wider context for it?

Checklist:

Key takeaways from this chapter are:
- Memories are shaped by the circumstance in which they are made.
- With context, painful memories can be softened.
- Careful and cautious analysis of our memories is an important way of addressing the pain they carry so that they don't dictate our decision-making process.
- It is our responsibility to create order out of the chaos of our past.

Action Plan:

- Spend some time every day writing down a few thoughts about memories.
- Pay attention to painful memories that seem to crop up out of nowhere and do not dismiss them immediately.
- Spend some time trying to find context for your memories, both painful and otherwise.

Rule 10: Plan and Work Diligently to Maintain the Romance in Your Relationship

The Unbearable Date

Jordan Peterson begins this chapter of *Beyond Order* with a caveat that he is not a couple's therapist but sometimes has to see clients with their partners. He sometimes suggests going on a date and is often met with a response that it will not go well, so they don't bother. But he suggests that with a little care and perseverance a couple can rediscover each other in new ways that they never thought possible before.

Bedrock

Sex, says Jordan Peterson, can say a bit about a relationship but not the whole story. There might be unaddressed issues in the relationship which do not manifest themselves in the bedroom. He explains that one should learn how to verbalize desire but to be aware that it gives your partner a source of power, which leaves you vulnerable. For sex to work, there must be trust.

Christ in the Candle

Peterson begins by looking at the Swedish Christian custom of the couple holding a lit candle between them when they get married. The symbolism is profound - the light against the darkness, and in the Christian tradition meant to symbolize Jesus Christ.

He interrogates the idea that, in a marriage, there is one subordinate and one dominant, and suggests that, instead, both are subordinate to the guiding principle that unites them. While there is much cynicism about the idea that there are such things as soul mates or in the biblical idea that man and woman were once of one flesh and must be rejoined in the Christian doctrine, Peterson explains there is also something profoundly mature about joining with someone in marriage to say, publicly: I am not leaving you.

Negotiation, Tyranny, or Slavery

One of the elements that are difficult to master in a relationship is the act of negotiation. Many simply choose to avoid it, preferring to prevaricate and bluster their way through the relationship avoiding important conversations. Peterson advises us to be persistent, though, regardless of how uncomfortable or upsetting it may seem to try and address difficult issues.

He explains that there are sometimes two defenses put up by those who want to avoid discussion. These are anger and tears, and he says that it takes someone who has 'integrated their shadow' to move past these defenses and get to the root of the problem.

He next addresses the cynicism with which modern relationships are often built. Many choose not to get married or have kids - which in his professional opinion is a biological imperative of young women and it is rare for women not to feel that urge. Young women should make a decision early because pregnancy and the ability to get pregnant aren't a foregone conclusion.

This lack of caution about what life can offer is an effect found in marriages that have stagnated. A careless choice here or there can have deeper ramifications in the long term, and the divorce courts are not something anyone can look forward to.

The Domestic Economy

Here, Peterson looks at domestic roles in the household and how a couple might address domesticity in a world that is largely abandoning traditional gender roles in the house. Without the benefit of these traditional roles, the hierarchy of responsibility can be difficult to negotiate. What it requires is a thorough discussion of practical and personal matters. You must embrace the mundanity of domestic life in order to move on with the romance. Peterson introduces us to the idea of functional unity, a state which may only be achieved through dialogue.

Finally: Romance

Peterson concludes with his thoughts on marital romance. He explains that sex is an important part of a functional marriage, but that it should not be an end in itself. When kids come along, it is often better to plan sex around your other commitments. But there must be an approach that treats your spouse or partner as though you are meeting them for the first time.

Goal:

Jordan Peterson continues *Beyond Order* by explaining his thoughts on marital bliss in this chapter. He looks at how we must treat our partners as constantly evolving individuals with constantly evolving needs. He interrogates how we should approach sex and the myriad of benefits that come with an open and mature dialogue regarding the bedroom. He moves on to the usefulness of established conventions such as marriage itself and the urge to reproduce and spends a little time explaining how important it is to address domestic issues as well as romance.

Lesson:

Activity 1:
In this chapter, Jordan Peterson places great importance on the need for dialogue in a relationship. If you are in a relationship, make a list of the subjects you have talked to your partner about in the last week. How many correlate with Peterson's list of sex, domestic arrangements, personal anecdotes, and romance?

Activity 2:
If you are not in a relationship, make a list of ideas you have about relationships that might not take into account the mundanity that often comes with long-term relationships or marriage. If you have a particular 'type', how will you aim to maintain that relationship when the first thrill of it has settled into domesticity? What chores are you prepared to undertake to keep the love of your life in your life?

Checklist:

Key takeaways from this chapter are:
- Relationships must be worked on persistently in order to be maintained.

- Individuals are constantly evolving and we must be prepared to meet the afresh every chance we get.
- Sex only works well when there is open and frank dialogue.
- Domestic arrangements are an important part of a strong partnership.

Action Plan:

- Be prepared to communicate in an open and frank manner with your partner.
- Understand that while domestic arrangements are not exciting, they are necessary and must be divided between you to create harmony.
- Do not be hasty when it comes to romance - be prepared that finding a partner is not simple and we cannot just live with anyone for the rest of our lives.

Rule 11: Do Not Allow Yourself to Become Resentful, Deceitful, or Arrogant

The Story is the Thing

Here, Jordan Peterson begins this chapter of *Beyond Order* by asking the question: can we understand our existence in a way that avoids the pitfalls of resentment, deceit, and arrogance? Part of what makes us take these low roads is the knowledge that there are often untapped or unrealized possibilities that remain beyond our reach. In order to come to terms with this eventuality, we must accept that it may well be part of our personal story not to attain certain things. But that doesn't remove the importance of the story itself.

The Eternal Characters of the Human Drama
The Dragon of Chaos

The first character that Peterson introduces us to is one that he mentions often through the book. The dragon, or the monster, is one of the most compelling of characters in any story, whether it is Moby Dick, Smaug, or Grendel. We are compelled, on an evolutionary level to pay attention to the greatest threat in a story, the predatory aspect which may cause the downfall of the hero with whom we identify.

Nature: Creation and Destruction

How we engage with nature, like how we engage with the threat of the dragon, is an evolutionary response. We associate the wilderness with beauty and danger in all its forms, and so it holds both terror and benevolence. The duality of nature is an intrinsic part of storytelling, in that most stories have an element that is creative and a counterpart that is destructive.

Culture: Security and Tyranny

Peterson looks at the dualistic role of culture as a framework, a structure in which a story can unfold. It is the rules of the fairytale kingdom, ruled either by a benevolent king or by rampaging tyrant. Our stories are ruled by how we see these authoritative structures. For those of us who are conservative, we may view our ruling class as benevolent, but those of us who are liberal may view them as tyrants. It is necessary, however, that we are able to develop a balanced view of the ruling class as possessing elements of both.

The Individual: Hero and Adversary

Here, again, Peterson presents a duality of the hero and his counterpart, the nemesis. How our particular heroes are presented will depend on how we perceive their relationship with the other characters in the human drama. We cannot hope for a perfect hero, but we can try to move them through the system without damaging it.

Resentment

Peterson asks here why it is that we so often fall prey to resentment. It isn't always due to laziness or ignorance - sometimes it is genuinely misfortune. There is a terrifying element of randomness about them that can seem incredibly unfair. All we can do, and all he advises his clients to do when such unkind acts of providence come their way, is meet such challenges head-on, accept that there is little we can do to control events, but we can control how we react. If we are as lucky as we are unlucky, we might just be able to tilt the odds back in our favor.

Deceit and Arrogance

At the beginning of this section, he explains that there are two forms of deceit: that of commission, whereby we do deceitful things knowing full well that they are wrong; and that of omission, whereby we merely do not act when we see that something wrong is happening and let it slide. These deceits are often justified by those who suffer from resentment, but there is also an element of arrogance that is necessary for them to feel justified in deceiving.

Commissions

Arrogance is, in part what compels one to reject the relationship between truth and goodness. It also allows the deceiver to believe that they can alter the structure of reality itself, often for selfish gains. Every time the deceiver succeeds, unfortunately, this arrogance will only increase. They will believe that the deceit has the ability to survive on its own as reality rights itself. Eventually, when confronted, the deceiver will claim justice as an ally, that the resentment that motivated them in the first place is justified and justifies the deceit.

Omissions

One of the major reasons why one might sit by as things that are wrong happen is nihilism. It is the attitude that everything is meaningless - another kind of arrogance that requires one to subscribe not so much to an ideology but an absence of ideology. Those who stand by might consider the lack of action as a justifiably easy path, either through a sheer desire for self-preservation or through a lack of confidence.

The Existential Danger of Arrogance and Deceit

Peterson explains that a life of deception and arrogance can inevitably lead to a life of being deceived. You warp your own ideas of reality and truth and can no longer navigate through the misfortunes that may cause resentment, and thus you begin to circle in a maelstrom of resentment deceit, and further resentment. You reinforce the neural networks which require you to function in a particular way, and eventually, your sole method is deceit. And when you are eventually caught out, there is likely to be at least a partial, if not total, mental collapse.

The Place You Should Be

Peterson concludes this chapter with a call for us to meet the challenge of our future and rise to the heights of our potential. We must believe that there is enough goodness in the world to dispel some of the horrors of existence and embrace, instead of resentment, deceit, and arrogance, a notion of gratitude and truth.

Goal:

Jordan Peterson uses this chapter of *Beyond Order* to explore methods of how we might avoid becoming unproductive or even harmful members of society. First, he looks at the core tenets of the stories we tell ourselves to adjust to the reality that life is not always fair and there are things that might cause resentment if we are not vigilant. He looks at the key characters of these stories and the dualistic nature of story characters. Further, he looks at the reasons for resentment and the types of deceit we engage in as we try to deal with our resentment, and the results such deceit can lead to.

Lesson:

Activity 1:
In this chapter, Jordan Peterson goes to some lengths to present us with a framework to view our lives as a story - not necessarily one in which we achieve all our heart's desires, but one in which the hero with which we identify might persevere. Drawing from the list of characters in the summary above, write out the characters in your personal narrative, in both their light and dark forms.

Activity 2:
The chapter is devoted to resentment and deceit. Reflect on your own life and write down, as an exercise in self-discovery, what resentments you harbor. Write down the methods you have undertaken, thus far, to combat or dispel your resentments.

Activity 3:
Many of us, at one time or another, have toyed with deceit, either of omission or of commission. Write down, in 150 words or less, a moment or event in which you engaged in an act (or inaction) of deceit.

Checklist:
Key takeaways from this chapter are: • Resentment can flow from things that are beyond our control. • We must be prepared for the randomness of suffering. • To deal with resentment takes deep understanding and a great deal of work. • Reminding ourselves of our personal story is a good way of building resilience in the face of unjust suffering. • Deceit is often accompanied by arrogance. • Deceit often begets further deceit, but must always inevitably fall as reality seeks to right itself.

Action Plan:
• Engage with any resentment you harbor as you would a story. • Allow yourself to grieve for the things that are now and forever out of your reach, but adapt to the new reality within the parameters you have been set. • Understand that whatever possibilities are not available to you, they are not available to others as well. • If you find yourself caught in a web of deceit, remember that arrogance is a form of self-deceit and whatever deception you are engaged in will eventually come out.

Rule 12: Be Grateful in Spite of Your Suffering

Down can Define Up

Jordan Peterson begins this concluding chapter of *Beyond* Order by explaining that he has searched for certainty for many decades, and has done so by process of elimination. He has tested and retested ideas he holds dear for structural weaknesses. He believes that suffering is an inevitable and shakable truth.

However, we might be able to blunt some of the sharpest edges of suffering by facing it courageously. Through challenging the darkness, we are inviting in the light, and as a consequence, gratitude.

The Mephistophelian Spirit

Here, he looks at Goethe's rendition of the Faust myth, and in particular the character of the lesser devil who tempts him, Mephistopheles. He is the adversary of the play, the representation of Faust's dark desires. For psychoanalysts, the revelation of the multiplicity of the human psyche was an important discovery, but also frightening in that it begged the question: who is in control if we are not always conscious of our darker selves?

Here, Peterson digresses into a wider conversation about how we struggle with these inner forces and attempt, often fruitlessly, to discover which recesses of our mind they reside. He likens it to the belief by some that to bring a child into a world that is so full of suffering is selfish. Such is the belief of those who commit suicide or even mass shootings in the case of Columbine, Peterson says.

However, Peterson explains that these beliefs must be held by the darker selves, the adversarial selves that resemble Mephistopheles as he tempts Faust towards hell. He explains that it is a human condition that he is very familiar with as a clinical psychologist.

But he also explains that such modes of bitterness serve no purpose, and it is of far greater benefit to be grateful and enjoy what one has rather than fall into despair.

Courage-But Superordinate, Love

In the final section, Peterson reminds us that where bitterness and resentment may present a temptation, it is only through a sense of courage and love that we might voluntarily choose an alternate path. It is a path that leads away from destruction and despair, but even further, allows us to play a part in keeping the world from degeneration.

We must accept that grief is a mere iteration of love, and it is often moments of grief where are presented with the option to choose despair or courage, and it is there that we may even excuse resentment as a natural process. But as we saw in the previous chapter, resentment is a spiral.

Further, that grief is an iteration of love means that we must hold on to that part which loves, and those which we love and lose are only made eternal by love, rather than resentment.

Goal:

This final chapter of *Beyond Order* by Jordan Peterson looks at the difficult and sometimes fruitless choices we must make when presented with moments of despair. He explains that it is an iteration of ourselves that chooses resentment and deceit, and is often capable of making them seem very attractive. Gratitude is hard, but is an embodiment of love, and can only be accepted for the rewards that love gives us. They are not attainments in the material sense, and only partially reduce the sting of loss - of a loved one, health, aspirations - but are a method by which we can appreciate those things that we have, be it memory, learning, or understanding that would not have otherwise gained were it not for suffering.

Lesson:

Activity 1:
In the spirit of this chapter, whatever mental state you are in, list out all the things you are grateful for. Try to think of the assets of your personality which make you a desirable, useful member of society and those which will continue to give you a sense of pride.

Checklist:

Key takeaways from this chapter are:
- Suffering must be faced.
- Further suffering is often inflicted by our darker selves.
- It is human to be tempted towards despair.
- We must seek courage and love to discover an alternative to resentment.

Action Plan:

- Be willing to confront the darker part of yourself, so that you may recognize it when it tempts you towards resentment.
- Do not allow yourself a moment of resentment.
- Find your courage by finding your love.
- Be grateful for what you love.

Quiz

1. What is Jordan Peterson referring to when he talks about 'social institutions'?
2. What are the ways in which an individual may move up and down the social hierarchy?
3. On what occasions is it acceptable to subvert social institutions?
4. Can both conservative and liberal ideologies co-exist?
5. What eminent myth cycle does Jordan Peterson like in the individual's journey towards a single-minded purpose?
6. Why are narratives useful when searching for purpose?
7. Are notions of the individual as 'the hero' a useful concept?
8. What does Peterson refer to when he talks about 'the Fog'?
9. How important are the irritations we face on a daily basis?
10. To whom is our greatest responsibility owed?
11. How might one go about challenging a harmful ideology?
12. What constitutes a moral obligation to challenge or remove yourself from a workplace or public space?
13. Why should we be wary of ideologues?
14. What is the difference between an ideology and a social institution?
15. How do parameters and constraints contribute to unleashing our potential?
16. What is the value of self-discipline?
17. Why is it important to learn how to work as part of a team?
18. Why is art important?
19. Why must we embrace the grotesque along with the beautiful?
20. What can we learn from children in terms of art?
21. How are memories shaped?
22. How can we address painful memories so that they do not impede our future?

23. What is the value of domestic arrangements in a cohabiting relationship?
24. What are the key characters that feature in the 'Human Drama'?
25. How must we challenge the 'Mephistophelian Spirit?

Thank You!

Hope you've enjoyed your reading experience.

We here at Genius Reads will always strive to deliver to you the highest quality guides.

So, I'd like to thank you for supporting us and reading until the very end.

Before you go, would you mind leaving us a review on Amazon?

It will mean a lot to us and support us in creating high-quality guides for you in the future

Warmly yours,

The **Genius Reads** Team

Manufactured by Amazon.ca
Bolton, ON

21820830R00044